Enjoy KiDS ABC

This book is suitable for children ages 4 and up

It is dedicated to teaching them how to write letters with one word for each letter

author : mohmed Abdullah

Aunt

B B B B B B

b b b b b b b b b

Book

Car

D D D D D D D D

d d d d d d d d

Dog

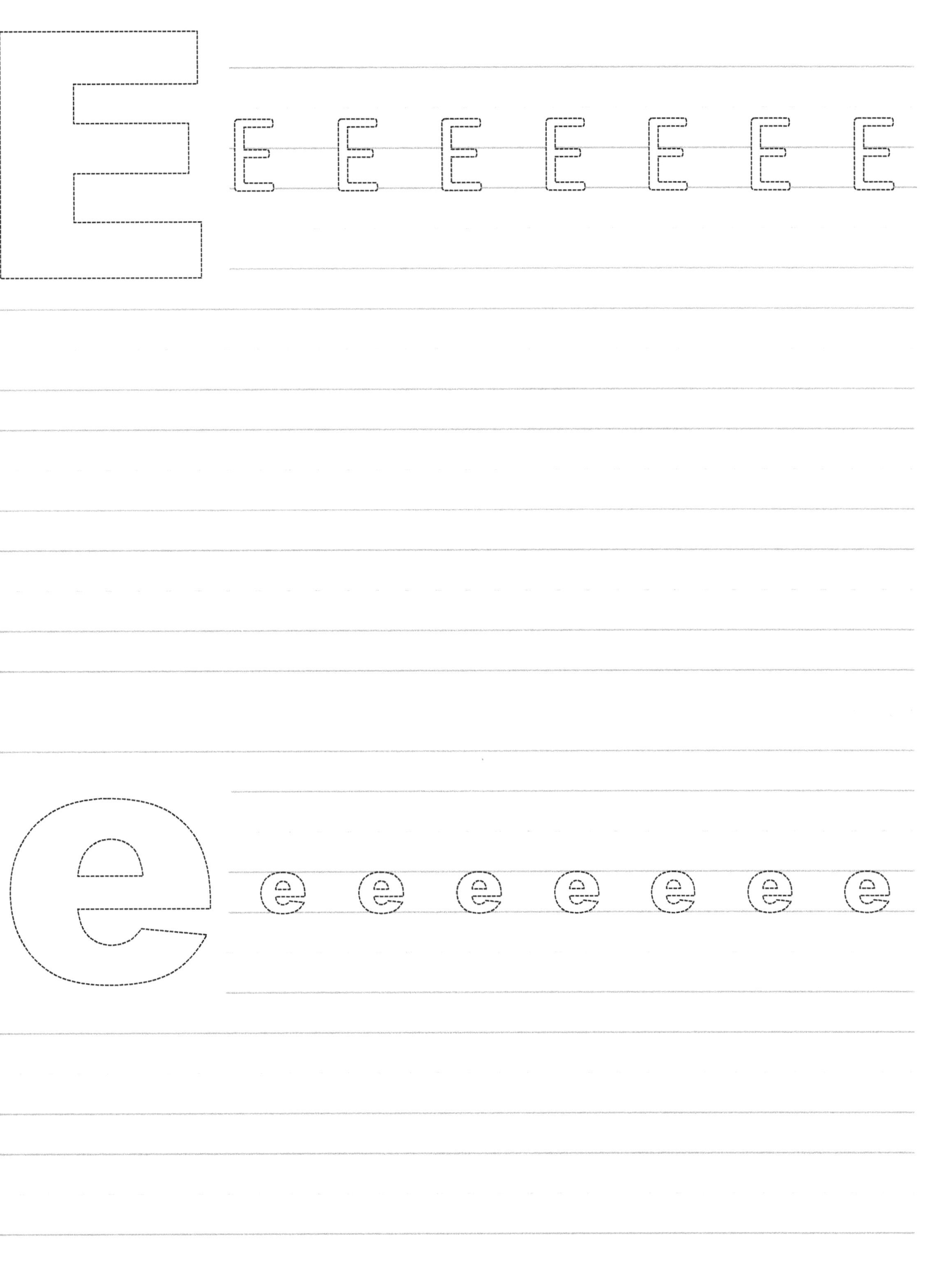

Elephant

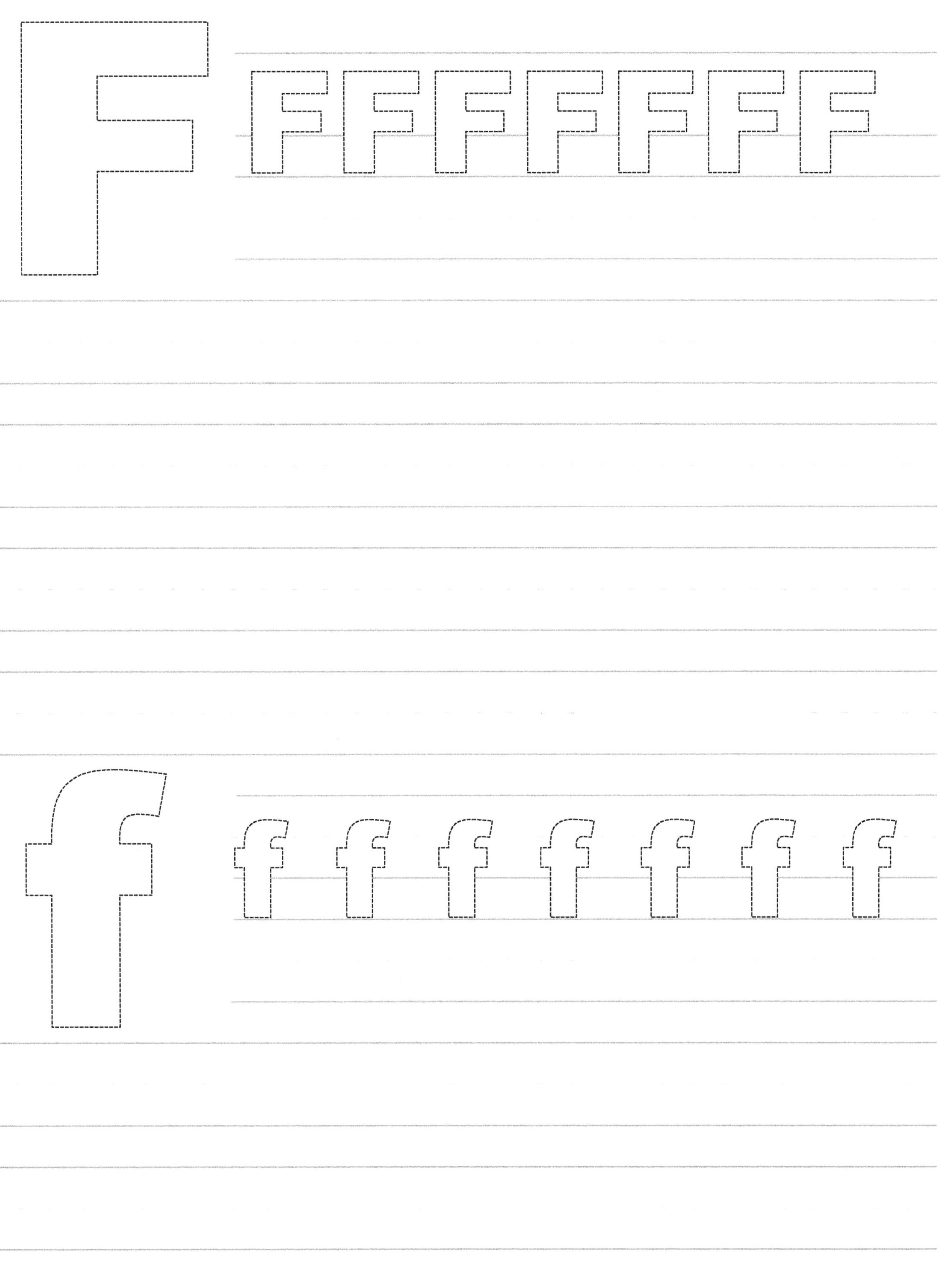

Food

Gorilla

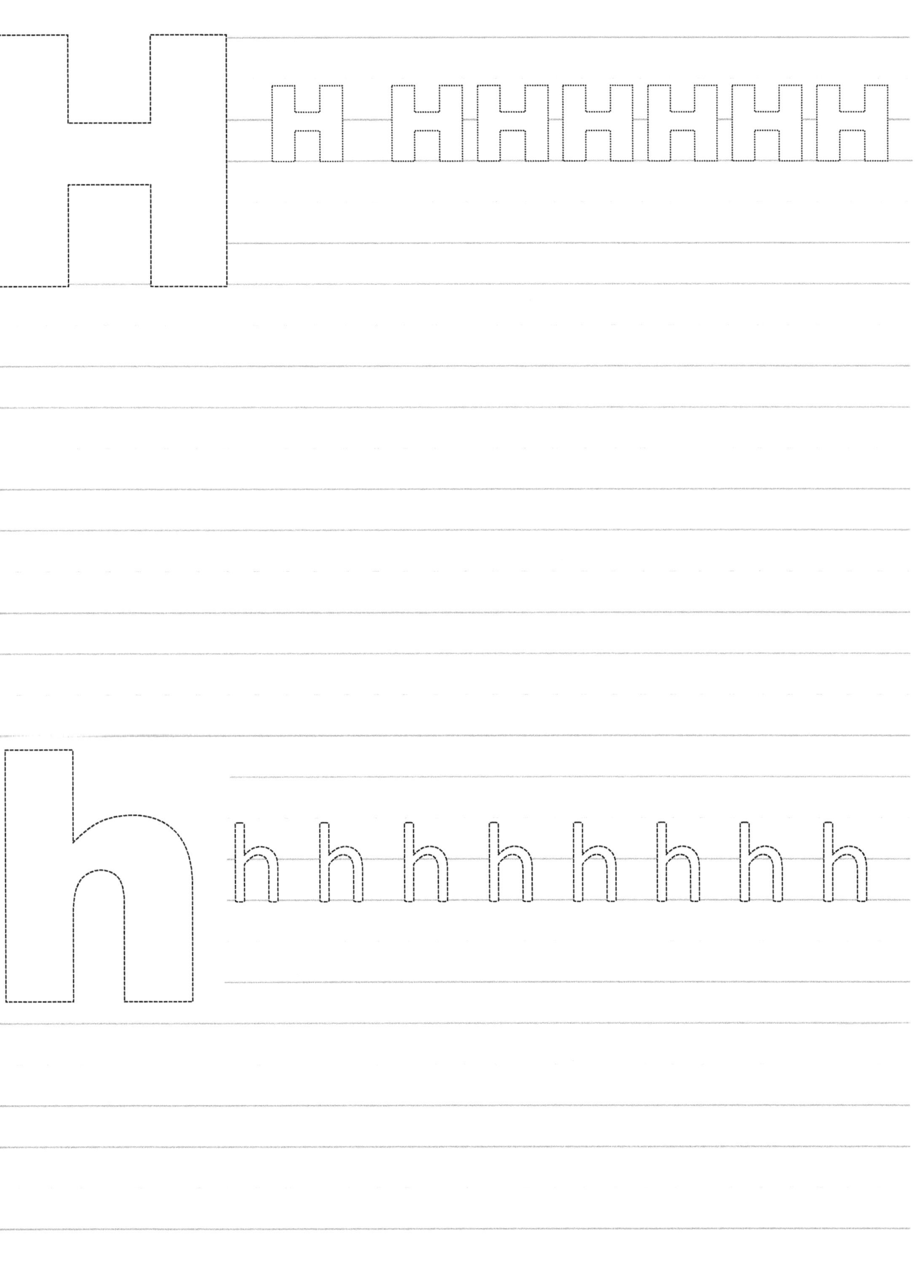

Home

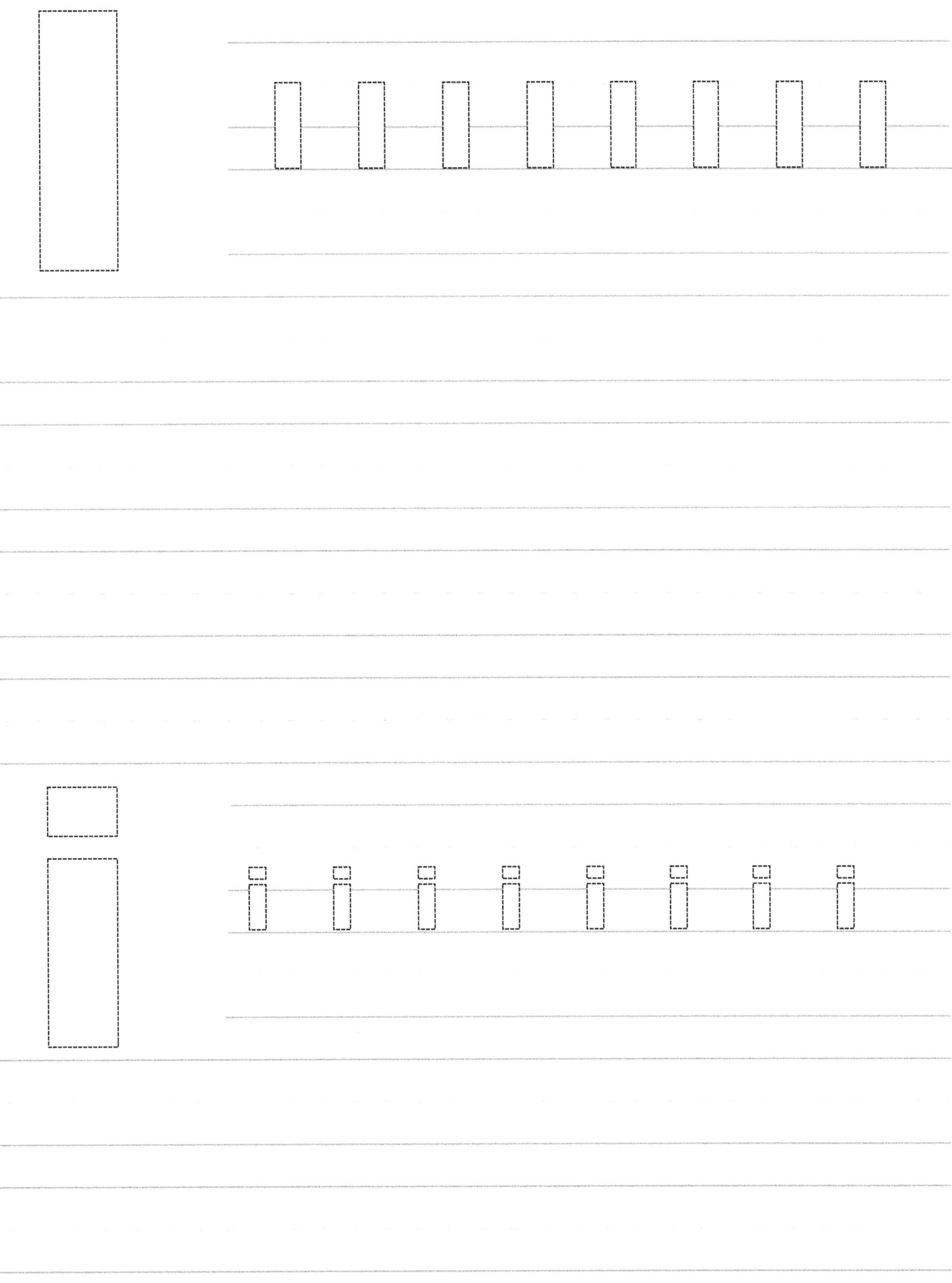

Island

Jocket

Kids

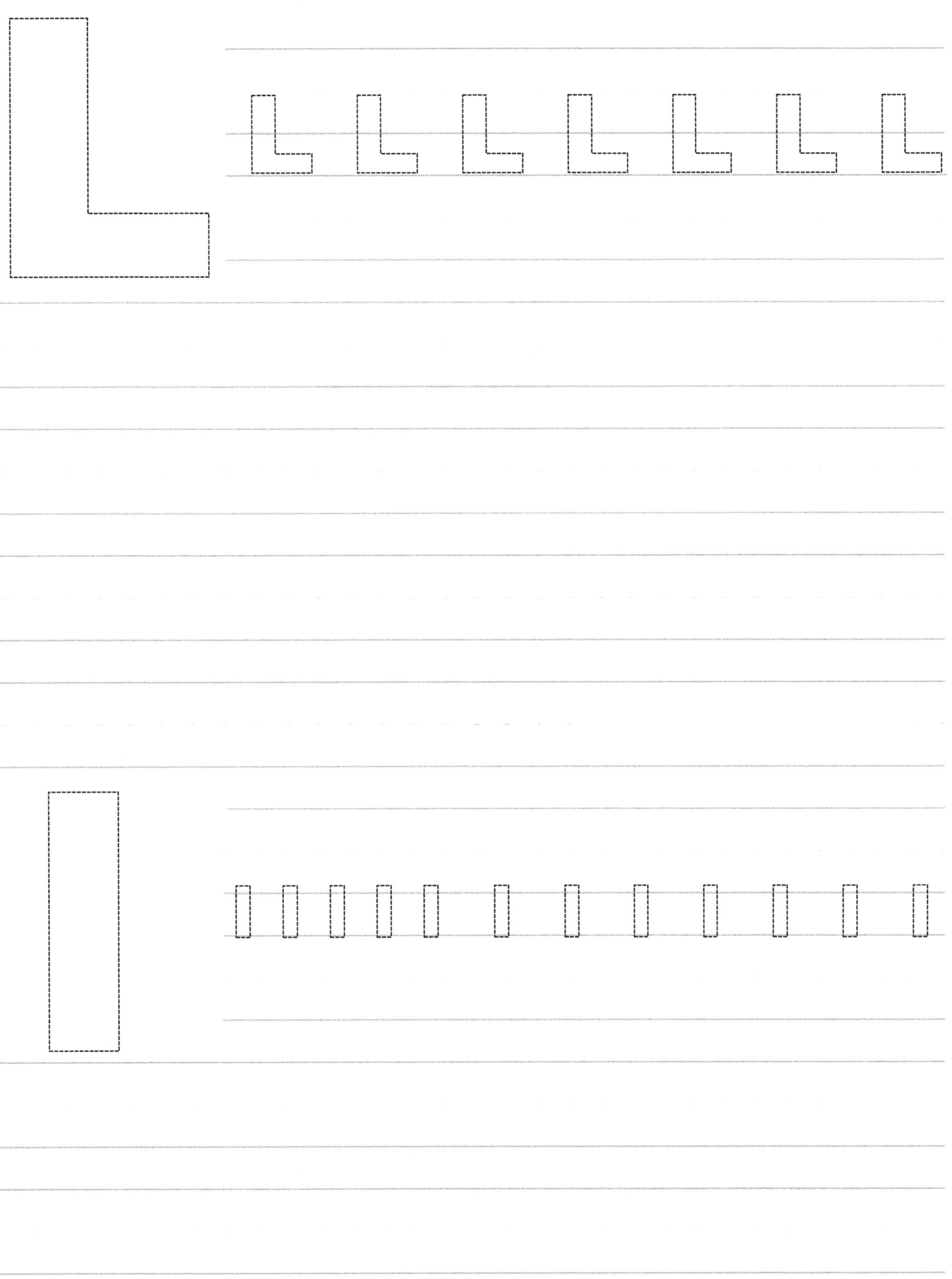

Leg

M M M M M M M

m m m m m m m

Moon

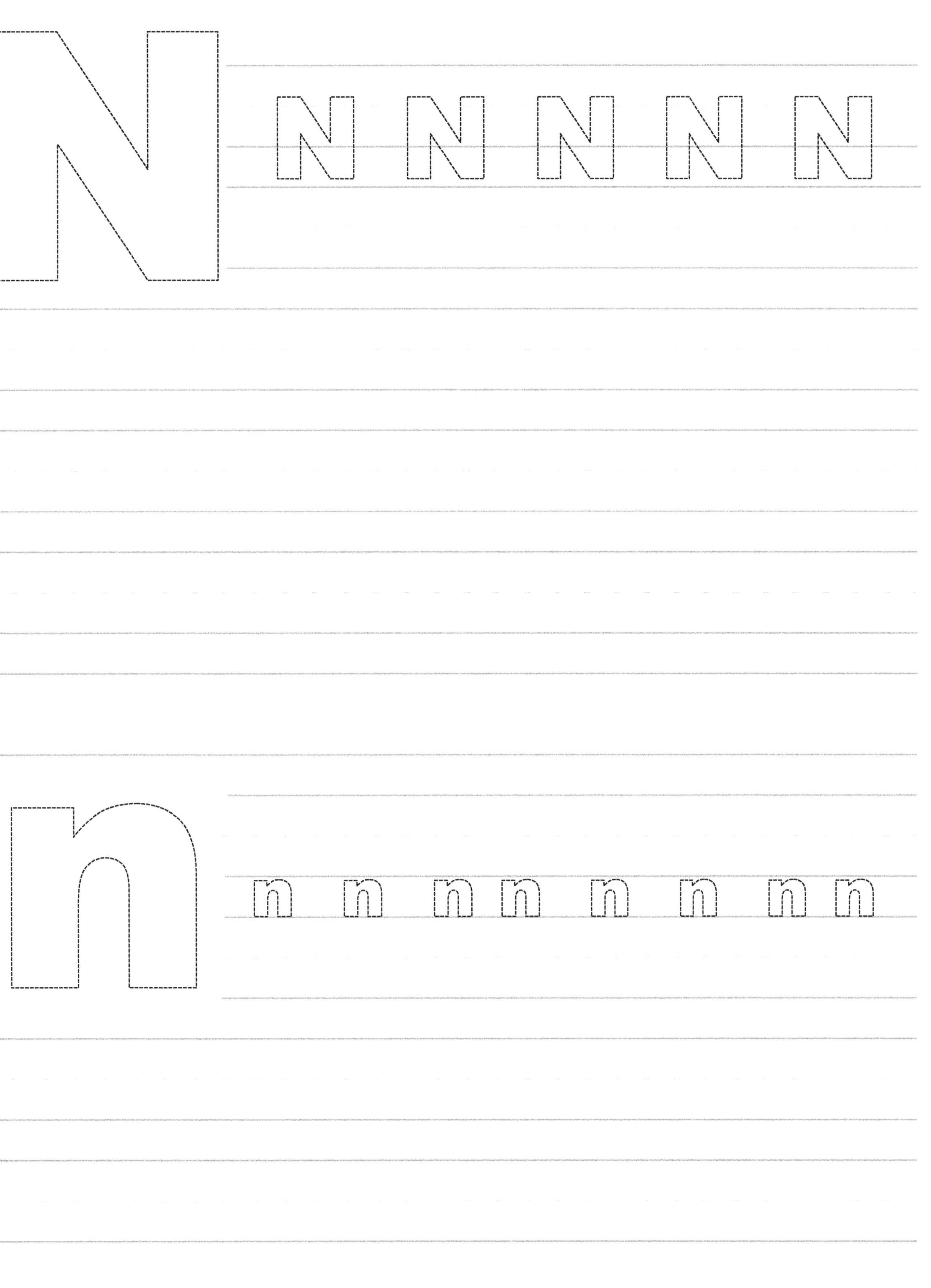

Noise

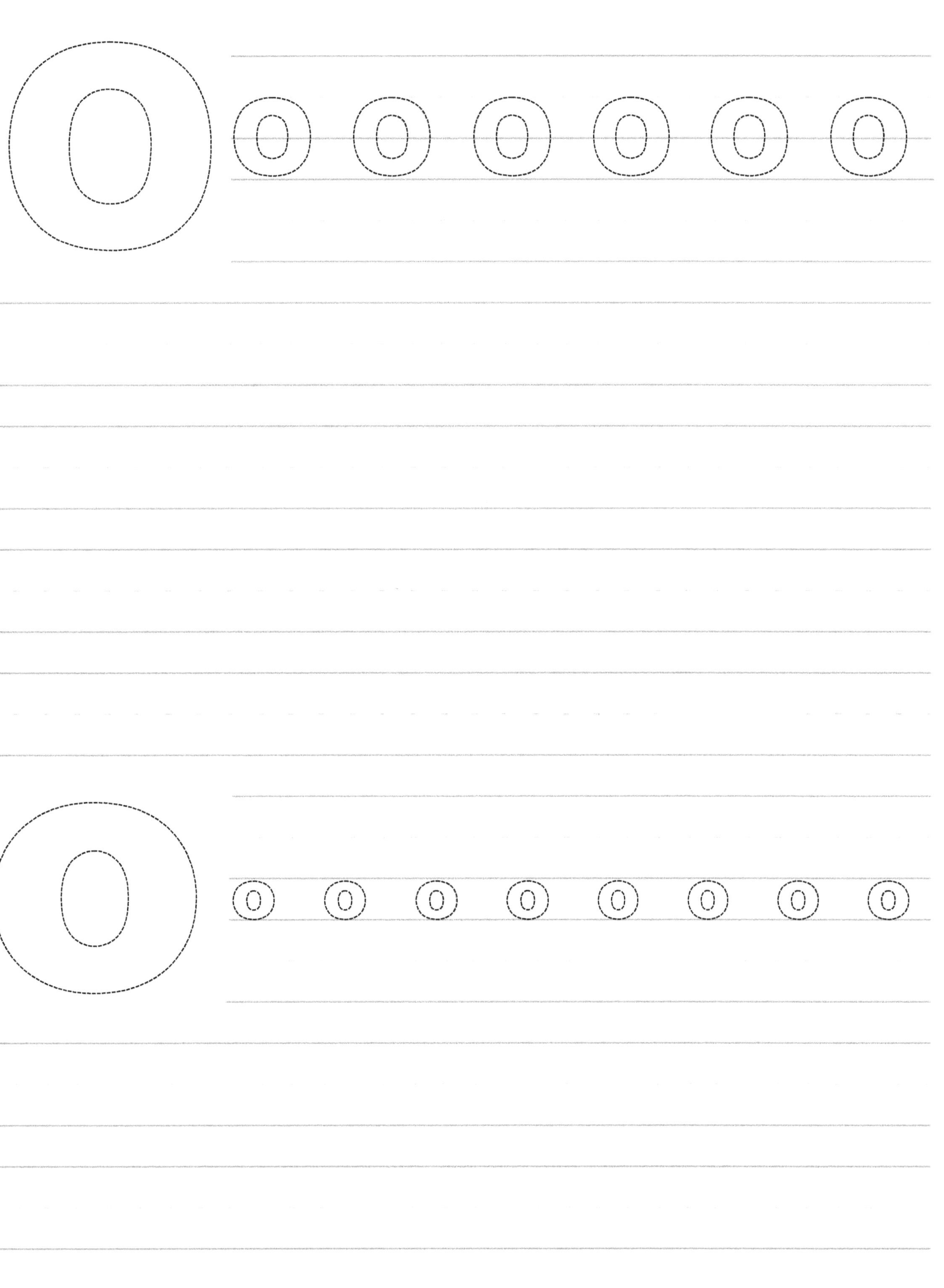

Orange

Poilt

Queen

Rabbit

Sea

Tree

Unicorn

Van

World

Xray

Yellow

zebra